Breaking Free

from the spirit of death

Jonathan Hunter

embracing
LIFE
MINISTRIES

Dedication

To Terry and Andrea Hunter who powerfully interceded for my life back in December 1979. The Lord answered your prayers and more. The evidence is found in these pages.

Foreword

I know of no better witness to Jesus' life sustaining and transforming power than Jonathan Hunter. When I first met Jonathan, he was young in faith yet already contagious in his zeal for Christ; he knew his life depended on Christ's life, a truth he sought early on to impart to anyone with ears to hear.

Emerging out of the domination of homosexuality was only the beginning for Jonathan. His HIV diagnosis provoked us all to discover new ways of doing battle amid Jonathan's temptation toward heaviness and despair. We knew that Jesus had redeemed Jonathan for a purpose other than a premature death.

Through that struggle to choose life in the face of his death sentence, Jonathan deepened as a man and as a minister. He discovered Jesus' capacity to sustain his very existence; over and over, he learned how Jesus displaced hopelessness with expectancy, even joy, over what He willed for the future.

Jonathan reflected light for all of us. His weakness became in God's hands a source of holy power for the Desert Stream staff. In our meetings, he would be the first to identify and lead the team in refusing the unbelief and worldly sorrow that would tempt us corporately. He provoked us to align ourselves with Life—Christ Himself—that we might rise afresh with Him to do His will.

God entrusted Jonathan with this key of life. It is reflected well in this booklet, and it has the power to reveal and cancel out the spirit of death. Countless ones have benefited from the Life described here. First Jonathan centered on the HIV-affected, then expanded its relevance to all those facing some kind of death sentence or another.

What compelled me most about this key of Life is the way in which even the physically sound are tormented in soul by the dark thoughts and feelings that shroud our view of the empty tomb. This results in our knowing the truth on one hand, and yet on the other hand, still living in darkness.

The truth set forth in the following pages is nothing less than a piercing apprehension of the resurrection—Jesus raised from the dead to put underfoot the power of death. Christ invites and enables us to do the same. Jonathan's life in Christ could be summarized accordingly. Over two decades after his HIV diagnosis, Jonathan continues to live the truth expressed in this booklet.

Heed the truth presented here. Refuse anything less than the Risen Christ. Live.

Andy Comiskey

Breaking Free... from the spirit of death

The people walking in darkness have seen a great light; on those living in the land of the shadow of death a light has dawned. Isaiah 9:2

But you are a chosen people, a royal priesthood, a holy nation, a people belonging to God that you may declare the praises of him who called you out of darkness into his wonderful light. 1 Peter 2:9

◆　　◆　　◆

I'll never forget the first time I heard Jonathan Hunter speak on the spirit of death. I was very tired and didn't want to go to his seminar, which was on a Saturday. Reluctantly I went.

At that time in my life, I had already received a great deal of healing. I had been in therapy for five years and, in my mind, had a very good sense of why I felt the things I felt and why I had the problems I had—some of which were stubborn. I'd received healing prayer many times. So I went to the talk with low expectations. Yet his lecture and the prayer time that followed changed my life altogether.

During the talk, I realized how pervasive fear was in my life. I didn't fear death as much as I wanted it; I realized that the desire to die that I'd indulged was sinful, and had opened the door to darkness. I feared many other things as well: possible sicknesses, tragedies and calamities. I had been sick a lot in my life and had come to expect illness. My belief was that my fears were psychological and would simply take time to eradicate.

At the end of this lecture, Jonathan had us renounce the spirit of death. As I did so, I had a small fit of coughing and began to cry a little. It was obvious that something was happening, but I didn't know what it was…until the next day.

It was like a thick, gray lens through which I'd seen reality had been removed from my heart. I no longer feared illness and calamity. I had hope for the good things God wants to give. I had hope for health, blessing and prosperity. I was stunned. It was hard for me to believe how dramatic the difference was. I've never been the same, psychologically or otherwise. Besides the new absence of fear, my health improved. Now, when I'm tempted to fear those things again I simply renounce and send away the spirit of death. And God has been faithful to give me the life He promised.

- M.P.

Contents

Introduction

You have made known to me the path of life... Psalm 16:11

> *I was still quite sick in my body, heavy inside with thoughts that this disease would always rob me of life. I still had hope that somehow and somewhere God would ease this condition in my body and also ease the pains still living in my heart and mind and spirit. I was depressed, hoping for more life, still carrying around accumulated hurts from my childhood and the Body of Christ. I knew many of God's truths in my head but was tired and weary for I knew they were not yet deep in my being. I needed God to help me more.*

Perhaps some of the sentiments expressed above are familiar to you— the despairing frustration, life always beyond your grasp. Though the woman quoted above does struggle with a physically debilitating illness, there is a deceitful, unnamed influence that entangles her life— and perhaps yours. Unmasked, it can be identified as the spirit of death.

A World in its Grip

The effective range of the spirit of death goes far beyond the chronically or terminally ill. Ours is a world where just about everybody is under its spell to some degree. A quick perusal of the newspaper or channel-surfing the TV confirms the fact: terrorist attacks, wars, racism, religious strife, gang activity, drugs, you name it—no person, no community, no nation is free from its influence. The right to exert its influence lies in the profoundly fallen state of the world we live in—a state that many learn to just live with. There are many historic, vivid examples of this kind of corporate enslavement by the spirit of death, including Nazi Germany, the Armenian genocide, slavery in America, Rwanda's Hutus and Tutsis, the treatment of Native Americans, all equally stunning and heinous and all evoking generational impact. However, it is not only physical manifestations or murder, but the battle over human thought life that comprises the main activity of the spirit of death. The most terrible, persistent conflicts remain confined to our minds—the unseen warfare within. That is where our confrontation lies, where true liberation and true peace must come.

Years of teaching and ministering on the subject all over the world has taught me that unknowing acceptance of the spirit of death is pandemic in the body of Christ. I first wrote about breaking free in the *Embracing Life Series (ELS)* guidebook, a healing, discipleship program for people with life-altering conditions. The teaching is only one of thirteen in the series; however, it remains the one that participants cite as most impacting their lives. The healing God brings through identifying, renouncing and resisting the spirit of death is dramatic. This booklet was published to give people a tool to help them break free from death's dreadful tyranny (and to also satisfy the high demand for this teaching previously only found in the *ELS* guidebook).

Although *Breaking Free from the spirit of death* deals with death and its influences, it is really all about hope and possibility. It is about the good news that we can be partakers of the fullness of life that is our inheritance in Christ Jesus. In this booklet, the emphasis is on getting free from the influence of the spirit of death, not just garnering more knowledge about it. My sincere hope and expectation for you who read this booklet is that after the concluding prayer, you'll be experiencing more freedom and life in Christ than when you first picked it up.

A Personal Odyssey of Discovery

Indeed, in our hearts we felt the sentence of death. But this happened that we might not rely on ourselves but on God, who raises the dead. 2 Cor. 1:9

In October of 1985, I tested positive for HIV, the AIDS virus. After three-and-a-half years of abstaining from sexual activity and drugs, this news came as quite a blow. Up until that time, I had naively believed that becoming a Christian automatically healed me of any damaging medical consequences from my previously promiscuous lifestyle. The counselor at the clinic informed me otherwise. "Nope," he said, "the virus is definitely there. You're infected alright."

I was shocked. I couldn't believe it. I numbly walked out to my car, my world now surreally turned upside-down. As I drove back to the office where friends were waiting, I cried out to God: "This is what I got saved for! What's so great about being born again... and infected! New creature in Christ? Big deal! You can't even get rid of a little virus! Where's the hope, the future? I'm dead meat now!" My whole body was burning from the emotional turmoil churning inside me. The thought of facing friends with the news made me feel sick.

My life as a Christian—a mere five years duration at the time—was in for a BIG growth curve. I had become a Christian back in 1980, shortly after recovering from an accidental drug overdose—and near-death experience—a resurrection only the power of God could have accomplished. I knew I'd been given a second chance. Years later, still emerging from the vestiges of my old gay identity and the shame and self-hatred associated with it, the diagnosis of HIV+ put me right back into the shadow of imminent death. The sudden prognosis presented

13

me with a new host of destructive thoughts that attacked my mind: feelings of despair, fear, intense anxiety and abandonment.

Gratefully, the persistent prayers from dear brothers and sisters helped quell the bombardment of those depressing thoughts. Substantive hope and peace began being restored. More and more, I learned to confront those deadly attacks when they occurred, by exercising my authority in Christ.

Just before I tested positive, I had begun volunteering with Desert Stream Ministries. At the same time, I continued to pursue an acting/modeling/waiting-on-tables career. Eventually, I came on fulltime as head of Desert Stream's AIDS outreach, originally called A.R.M., and later renamed Embracing Life.

It seemed like I sort of stumbled into AIDS ministry. I had no special training, medical or ministerial. I just knew there was hope for people with AIDS and God loved them. Hey! My testimony was proof of that. I was more aware of the psychological motives I had for pursuing acting. I had been in it for years—a long time to reflect on why I was driven to do what I did. The motives were not profound or unique: the need for affirmation and acceptance, escape into fantasy, the applause, stardom...everything you've heard from actors before.

Christian ministry was different and so were the issues (psychological and spiritual) that came up while doing AIDS work. What would eventually become the most crucial one—the presence of the spirit of death—didn't surface until several years after the ministry started. That discovery began unfolding at a prayer meeting one night when Andy Comiskey (see foreword on page 5) suggested with some concern that I appeared unfazed by a string of recent deaths of several AIDS patients. I reacted defensively and was just a little bit insulted. Inside I was thinking: "Hey! Who are you to be questioning how I'm reacting? I don't see you doing this work!" I replied with something like, "I'm just used to death, that's all. Anyway, it's enough to know they're with the Lord, in heaven." It was suggested I might be just "a little overly-familiar with death."

Awash in self-doubt and confusion, I left. All the way home I questioned the Lord and myself: "Was Andy right? I thought I had a 'gift' for tolerating death around me? Was there something(s) in my childhood, family, generational stuff that was surfacing? God, am I cold-hearted? What's going on here?"

The ensuing months proved pivotal in my life and for the ministry. The Lord kept bringing to mind one memory after another revealing a major pattern in my life—of making false peace with death. The most difficult times came, however, when pride would try to prevent me from honestly naming it. Finally, I had to name and confront it for what it was—DEATH—and command it to leave. When old thought and feeling patterns would re-emerge, I'd complain, "Surely I don't have to do this again!" Then, with each confrontation, if I stopped to listen, the Lord's words would come to mind: "I have come that they may have life, and have it to the full" (John 10:10). One thing I knew for sure—I hadn't yet tasted enough life to satisfy me. I wanted more! Freedom and determination came from the hunger for more: "Taste and see that the Lord is good..." (Ps. 34:8).

There were many layers of falsehood about life and God to get through. Evil was never named in my family. As I thought back on my childhood, it never entered my thoughts—or likely my parents'—that there might be spiritual strategies against my life. To my knowledge, my parents didn't have an in-depth relationship with Christ, so Jesus' help was never requested when trouble occurred. The subject of death was never discussed. In my senior year of high school my mother and two friends died. There was no one who was available or who offered to help me sort through the painful loss and confusion. I had to deal with it on my own. A succession of deaths, followed. My own near-death experience from the drug overdose left an indelible impression on my soul. My family's multi-generational denial and avoidance of the subject of death assured I'd be reticent to confront it. Given the numerous ways my mind and heart had been influenced by death, the Lord graciously revealed the truth at a pace I could deal with. Little by little, He gave me understanding of how the enemy's schemes and deceit had kept me in the dark when it came to experiencing true Life.

Unmasking the spirit of death

The enemy pursues me, he crushes me to the ground; he makes me dwell in darkness like those long dead. Psalm 143:3

The term "spirit of death," may be foreign to some. I have come to define it as a spiritual influence, a shadow over our days that veils the way we view life, subverts our perceptions and shapes a fatalistic mindset. It is not actual physical death that results from accident, disease or old age, although that is part of its design and consequence, but rather the spiritual essence and atmosphere of a fallen world emanating from "The God of this world." As stated in 1 John 5:19, "the whole world is under the control of the evil one."

Charles H. Kraft, prominent author, professor (Fuller Theological Seminary) and minister in the area of inner healing and deliverance, has observed a hierarchy of sorts with spirits. The spirit of death commands many other dark forces. Under this spiritual general, a constellation of other spirits work to destroy a person's life—all of them ultimately serving the evil one, Satan.

As Christians, we know there are two kingdoms (Mt. 12:25-28): one of light, one of darkness; one of life and one of death. In Colossians 1:13, we read that the Father has "qualified us to share in the inheritance of the saints in the kingdom of light. For he has rescued us from the dominion of darkness and brought us into the kingdom of the Son he loves" (Col. 1:12,13). Or said another way, he has "delivered us from the power of darkness, and hath translated us into the kingdom of his dear Son" (KJV). The spirit of death seeks to keep us ignorant of the rights and promises that have come with that transaction, igniting an inner dialogue involving the old or false self and/or the enemy.

Destructive voices try to eliminate, refute or ignore Christ's promises of ever-increasing life. Indeed, preceeding the Lord's promise of abundant life in John 10:10, he states, "The thief [Satan] comes only to steal and kill and destroy." Our enemy's minions and systemic propaganda accentuate thoughts of death and destruction, i.e., helplessness, hopelessness, and worthlessness. Death's "bad news" opposes the liberating gospel of the cross and the fullness of life that Jesus Christ provides. However, unlike the Lord, the devil is not omnipresent. Whenever we sense this deadly presence, we can assume in most cases that we are not being harassed by Satan himself, rather, it is an atmosphere of death, influenced by demonic strongholds and supported by cultural and personal belief systems, that is most likely besetting us.

The term "spirit of death" best describes (for our purposes) the influential effect of all of death's manifestations—the feeling of separation from God. Some familiar and similar terms can be found in scripture: "darkness," "the power of the grave," "days of darkness," "sentence of death," and "spirit of despair." Isaiah 25:7 speaks of, "...the shroud that enfolds all peoples, the sheet that covers all nations." Isaiah 9:2 alludes to "the shadow of death," as does Psalm 23.

Land of Shadow

Psalm 23

The Lord is my shepherd, I shall not be in want.
He makes me lie down in green pastures
He leads me beside quiet waters, he restores my soul.
He guides me in the paths of righteousness for his name's sake.
Even though I walk through the valley of the shadow of death,
I will fear no evil, for you are with me;
Your rod and your staff, they comfort me.
You prepare a table before me in the presence of my enemies.
You anoint my head with oil; my cup overflows.
Surely goodness and love will follow me all the days of my life,
And I will dwell in the house of the Lord forever.

The psalm is a personal favorite of mine because of its powerful imagery and compressed drama. In effect, the reader is taken on a telescopic lifetime journey with the Lord. The psalmist's words speak right to the heart, particularly the "valley of the shadow of death" part. Placed in the middle of the psalm, hope and fulfillment hinge on the shepherd's ability to get David (and you and me) through that all-too-familiar place of foreboding. Of course, He does, although for many, that truth is hard to grab hold of.

It is easy to get fixated on the valley because it so evocatively describes that place on the sojourner's road of life where one often feels stranded—four flat tires, no cell phone, no Auto Club card, no help in sight. Some of us, because of the ongoing difficulties and pain as we grew up, feel like we were raised in that "valley of the shadow." As one person put it: "Our family creed was, 'We are acquainted with grief.'" It is a legacy from our parents and we're resigned to it being our lot in life. Sure the location is depressing, but it is real estate! Years of living in that threatening emotional and spiritual place drives some to the erroneous conclusion that it is the Lord's will that they remain there, though nothing could be further from scriptural truth.

It is intended we pass "through" the valley; the Lord never purposed us to remain there. Having passed through it, however, doesn't exempt us from future valley excursions. Jesus exhorts us: "In this world you will have trouble. But take heart! I have overcome the world" (John 16:33). Jesus is the true shepherd of the psalm; His rod and staff bring comfort. Viewed as symbols representing His cross, the rod signifies Christ's authority, protection, guidance and rescue; the staff, in turn, represents the horizontal of the cross, for us the load bearing support of the Lord throughout our journey in life.

Comforting as those words are, for some of us the Lord's goodness noted in the verses surrounding "the valley" is obscured by the ominous "shadow of death"...despite the presence of the Shepherd. Our frustration is compounded by the shame we experience when, as Christians, we can't summon up an overcoming attitude. This psalm is a good diagnostic tool for unmasking the spirit of death in our lives, revealing to what degree we are living in its shadow, and ultimately leading us to "life."

Reflection & Meditation

Have you ever noticed how many people cite this as one of their favorite psalms? There's a reason: people relate to it. What impresses you most about it?

Meditate on the words of this psalm, one line at a time. Listen for the Shepherd's voice. Jesus said: "My sheep listen to my voice; I know them, and they follow me" (John 10:27).

Christians Under the Influence

Since the children have flesh and blood, he too shared in their humanity so that by his death he might destroy him who holds the power of death—that is, the devil—and free those who all their lives were held in slavery by their fear of death.
Heb. 2:14,15

If we belong to God, how can our lives be influenced, held back, strangled, cut off by this spirit of death? What about the scriptures that proclaim "if the Son sets you free, you will be free indeed" (John 8:36) and "the old has gone, the new has come" (2 Cor. 5:17)? What about Christ coming to "proclaim freedom for the captives" (Isa. 61:1) and so on?

A combination of factors make us vulnerable: Not knowing what Christ accomplished on the cross or the authority we have as believers; passivity; emotional, mental and verbal habits; unconfessed sin; inner vows and unforgiveness, among others. It is as if we had lived in a broken-down hovel. Then we came into a relationship with God through Christ and were given the deed to a mansion with a beautiful garden and all that goes with it. We either never realized what we'd been given or for some reason, when we made the move, we took our old trappings, furniture, and clothing with us (all the old perceptions, feelings, beliefs, twisted and formed by a spirit of death). Hence we couldn't experience fully what we'd been given. John and Paula Sanford have said "human free will is so precious to our Lord that he will not let the efficacy of the cross be applied to us without our consent."

This reminds me of a cartoon I find particularly apt that shows a dog chained to its tiny doghouse. In the background, one can make out the large house of the owner. A mesmerized cat sits next to the dog hanging on to its every word. The caption has the dog saying: "They don't keep YOU on a leash because they WANT you to run away." It is an amusing picture of our predicament. The dog (Satan for our purposes) is on a leash. The cat (representative of many a Christian) is clearly free to roam at will, to go in and out of the house (our heavenly Father's), yet is deceived by the cunning and lies of an envious enemy. Not exercising its privileges (and authority) to walk away free, the cat (us) remains in proximity of peril.

Why it Gets to Us

"He was a murderer from the beginning, not holding to the truth, for there is no truth in him. When he lies, he speaks his native language, for he is a liar and the father of lies." John 8:44

This deadly deceit can affect us in profound and personal ways by keying into our diseased thought patterns and habits. The enemy, the deceiver is familiar with human fallenness in all its forms. He should be; he was there at its inception in the Garden of Eden! Our enemy and his servants use that inside information to taunt us, lie to us and slander us at any given moment. He is the deceiver. Unfortunately, we are only too ready to agree with him. Unless our false ways of thinking and resulting actions are confronted, named, repented of and consistently renounced, our relationship with the Lord and our quality of life will continue to suffer. Unhealed, distorted and erroneous thoughts about God, identification with depression, anxiety, rejection, self-hatred, loneliness, hopelessness, despair, death fantasies etc., these all consume a tremendous amount of time, energy and imagination—mind matter. They are collectively a "house made of thoughts," as author Francis Frangipane describes them— creative space the Lord would rather occupy with Himself, i.e. LIFE. The dismantling of old thought structures cannot be a passive exercise; we have to participate with the Lord in their undoing.

When it Begins

The tongue has the power of life and death. Proverbs 18:21

The origins of our perceptions and imaginings (good or bad) go back to our childhood for the most part—memories forgotten or repressed, including how, when, where and from whom we got them. The immense impact of words and pronouncements (blessing and cursing) from adults who raised us and taught us, compounded by remarks from our peers, cannot be overstated. Our sponge-like souls absorbed everything we heard; we believed what was said about us was true. Life was straightforward and literal to our undiscerning minds. Hurtful names, so lightly tossed out in spite by others, seared our personhood. Harmful words created havoc with our internal perceptions of self: idiot, klutz, bastard, whore, slut, good-for-nothing...the list goes on and on. In the *Three Battlegrounds*, Frances Frangipane observes:

> *Their thoughtless words went so deep that, in recoiling from the pain, you have involuntarily remained in the recoiled or withdrawn position. Since then, you have refused to place yourself where you can become vulnerable to criticism. You may not even remember the incidents, but you may not have stopped recoiling, even until today.*

Poisonous words wound the soul and accumulate in the mind occupying ever-increasing space. Over time, they become an interior fortress of sorts; the price paid for its maintenance is a severe tax on one's well being. This formidable collection casts a shadow of bitterness and disappointment over gifts and sacraments the Lord intended to convey life. Words that God intended to impart comfort and assurance, to reflect his steadfast commitment and love, begin to carry a negative connotation after passing through our experiential grid:

Birth	"I (they) wish I had never been born."
Family	"It was never safe. We always Fought."
Marriage	"Entrapment."
Home	"It was a house I couldn't wait to leave."
Intimacy	"If they really got to know me, they'd reject me."

In my life, there were many areas that were fuel for disappointment: a confused sexual identity, unhappily married parents, alcoholic father, drugs, death of friends and mother, HIV infection, and a multi-generational pattern of illness, suicide and unacknowledged sin—strongholds for the spirit of death.

Depression, chronic illness, self-hatred, introspection, hopelessness, and self destruction associated with the spirit of death can result from a variety of experiences: birth traumas (being the child of rape, an unwanted pregnancy or failed abortion); suicide attempts; crippling or isolating childhood diseases; violent or emotionally abusive homes; caring for chronically ill family members; death of cherished loved ones; witnessing or having deadly tragedies happen to you, your immediate/extended family or ethnic group; rejection because of faith and gender; and countless other life-altering events or situations. Many who would appear to have had very happy childhoods and lives, may also have been just as affected. It's how we experience reality distorted by unredeemed thinking that causes us to fall prey to living in the valley of the shadow of death.

Reflection & Prayer

In the book of Ezekiel (18:32), the Lord says, "For I
take no pleasure in the death of anyone...Repent and
live!" What does that tell you about God's regard for
humanity? Since it's obvious God's will for you is life,
where are you making an accommodation for the
spirit of death in your thinking or actions? Ask God to
reveal it.

*Father, redeem my past. Help me to see relationship,
family, home, intimacy, marriage, (my) birth, through
your eyes. Resurrect my vision for life. Replace the
pronouncements and curses spoken over me by those
in authority and by my peers with your words of truth.
I wait on you.*

Operating Under the Influence

So many of us grow up viewing God's creation through a cloud of unbelief, cataracts that prevent us from perceiving and experiencing life more fully. Our over-identification with dark thoughts and faulty religious assumptions about God reinforce a jaundiced world-view resulting in impoverished relationships (beginning with God) and enfeebled ministries. It is no wonder the world is unimpressed by so much of what we're about as Christians; we go about life with such low expectations.

It is a sad irony that many serving in the helping professions—notably those working at hospitals, convalescent centers, in hospice care, social services and the like—are frequently the ones who least suspect they are under death's influence. That is precisely because they are under it. (Refer to my testimony in the Introduction.) You may have a familiarity with sickness, be drawn to help those more ill than you are, or an ability to tolerate death. These may seem good grounds for choosing a career as a caregiver, therapist or medical professional, but, unfortunately, our best intentions may be misinformed.

We need to look at our motives and impetus. Are our choices made out of an abundance of life in Christ, or because of our identification with things associated with death? Proverbs 16:2 says: "All a man's motives seem innocent to him, but motives are weighed by the Lord." So often they are tied in with our desire to make right what went wrong in our childhood. However, if we are willing to go before the Lord for an examination of our inner motivations, we might be surprised at what He uncovers.

Reflection & Prayer

Take some time to reflect on the reasons you chose the profession you did. Was it "a calling" from God? For primarily financial reasons? For personal healing, family business, a natural gifting...? How might your upbringing have influenced your career choice? Also consider: Are my relationships balanced? Have I chosen friends who are growing in their ability to embrace life or am I predominantly surrounded by those in the grip of death?

Father, show me the places where I live in the shadows and not your light. Search my heart and know me and reveal my motivations. I believe in your redemption from death. Help my unbelief. Reveal your love in a deeper measure to me and free me to love you with abandon.

Breaking Free

If you abide in My word, you are My disciples indeed, and you shall know the truth and the truth shall set you free.
John 8:31,32

Familiar fearful thoughts have convinced a lot of us that to take up arms against our foe will only lead to disappointment and failure, maybe even harm. Convinced of this lie, many of us have become spiritually apprehensive and sedentary when it comes to exercising our authority in Christ. Because we Christians have the potential of doing the most damage to the enemy, immobilized is exactly how the devil wants to keep us!

Getting free is not a simple one-time act or prayer, though the answer and means for achieving it can be simply put—Jesus Christ. The liberation we seek is and will be a process, an ongoing and progressive one achieved with the Lord. Getting free is all about Christ's authority in us. It says in Proverbs 9:10: "The fear of the Lord is the beginning of wisdom and *knowledge of the Holy One is understanding*" (emphasis mine). Implied here is the necessity for an intimate, abiding experience (union) with the Holy Spirit. Indeed, we must habitually nurture our relationship with the Lord of life before we can effectively recognize and overcome the spirit of death. As C. S. Lewis writes in his book *Miracles*, this is possible because of what the Lord has already done:

> *He is the first fruits, the "pioneer of life". He has forced open*
> *a door that has been locked since the death of the first man.*
> *He has met, fought, and beaten the King of death. Everything is*
> *different because He has done so.*

By His Strength and Authority

Jesus said, "I am the way, the truth and the life." John 14:6

"I am the Living One; I was dead and behold I am alive for ever and ever! I hold the keys of death and Hades." Rev. 1:18

It is all about the authority and strength of Christ to deliver us from destructive ways, just as St. Paul writes: "I can do all things through Christ who strengthens me" (Phil. 4:13 NKJV).

Dr. Charles Kraft has written extensively on the authority of Christ, emphasizing the necessity for Christians to understand and utilize that authority to live free from demonic harassment. In his books and seminars he often recounts the story of a woman who had been deeply involved in the occult and later became a Christian. She was able to share some valuable insights into occult activity and abilities. Most occultists, she said, understood and exercised the power they knew they possessed. Furthermore, they could "see" in the spirit realm those who didn't—namely Christians. They took special pleasure in intimidating unsuspecting Christians on the street with a look or a shove. However, she noted, every so often they would spot trouble coming—someone clearly aware of their authority in Christ. She, and those like her, took pains to avoid anyone who walked in that authority, even crossing to the other side of the street to get out of their way.

Since the birth, death and resurrection of Jesus Christ, the conflict with death has taken on new dimensions. A regenerated humanity has appeared on the field—God's enlistment to bring about His ultimate victory. No longer able to helplessly claim, "I'm only human," humanity has been given Godly strength in union with Christ. Through the Holy Spirit, God's mighty power is at work within to rebuff, attack and expel ungodliness. The apostle Paul models this new identity (as God's warrior) in his letter to the church at Corinth: "We demolish arguments and every pretension that sets itself up against the knowledge of God, and we take captive every thought to make it obedient to Christ" (2 Cor. 10:5). Paul's use of the present tense tells us that the encroachment of ungodly thoughts and ideas is an act of attempted control we humans must continually battle albeit with Christ. Again, to the Corinthians: "For He must reign [through us] until He has put all His enemies under His feet. The last enemy to be destroyed is death" (1 Cor. 15:26).

It is important to note that elsewhere, as in James 1:14,15, we read how our *willful* choices, consciously or not, can prolong the conflict: "But each one is tempted when he is drawn away by his own desires and enticed. Then, when desire has conceived it gives birth to sin; and sin, when it is full-grown, *brings forth* death." [emphasis mine] Indeed, there is an enemy on the prowl looking for the right moment to move in. Thus our fallen ways of thinking, believing and acting bring forth our enemy, giving him the right to harass us! We cannot afford to be passively resistant in the face of such attacks. We must "Resist him, standing firm in the faith" (1 Peter 5:8,9).

No matter who we are, we all come up against the presence of death in some form or another. Paul alludes to feeling "the sentence of death" in his heart. What we see repeated over and over in these scriptures is God revealing our weakness in the face of sin and death, and our need to be fully dependent on Him for redemption and deliverance.

Prayer

Father of Glory, give to me the spirit of wisdom and revelation in the knowledge of Christ. Let the eyes of my understanding be enlightened, that I may know what is the hope of your calling and what are the riches of the glory of Christ's inheritance in me, and what is the exceeding greatness of your power toward me and those who believe, according to the working of your mighty power which you worked in Christ when you raised him from the dead and seated him at your right hand in the heavenly places, far above all principality and power and might and dominion, and every name that is named, not only in this age, but also in the age which is to come (Eph. 1:17-21).

Staying Free

He has delivered us from such a deadly peril and He will deliver us. On Him we have set our hope that He will continue to deliver us, as you help us by your prayers. 2 Cor. 1:10,11

"For I know the plans I have for you," declares the sovereign Lord, "plans to prosper you and not to harm you, plans to give you hope and a future." Jer. 29:11

Repeat When Necessary

I've seen countless individuals set free from the contaminating torment that held them for so long. Once out from under that oppressive yoke, they begin their awakened life by making death their enemy (as it is to Christ). They continue to do so by repeatedly renouncing the spirit of death whenever they sense its familiar influence encroaching upon their lives. That is how one attains and sustains freedom from its effects, along with the obvious need for resting in God's strength, love and authority. Being creatures of habit, however, we all too quickly fall back into familiar, destructive ways of framing our perceptions and opinions about circumstances and people. It takes persistence in prayer and a resolute God-empowered will to live free from those old influences. The following is a brief testimony from one who has learned the process of getting free:

> *I had renounced the spirit of death numerous times, particularly as it related to my struggle with self-hatred and various fears. Recently, the Lord brought back to mind a season when I was bulimic. In the prayer time, I saw that I partnered with the spirit of death in my self-destruction. I had never truly repented of this. As I grieved over my sin, one particular memory was incredibly clear. In it I saw the cross very near me. The Lord invited me to turn to the cross—to*

Him—rather than to my self-destructive coping mechanisms. I had the choice between life and death. Though I had chosen death, He was offering me the opportunity to repent and choose life. I then asked the Lord what could be done about the inner pain that was driving my bulimia. Kneeling beside me, He said I wasn't meant to bear the pain. But He was. I could lean into Him and He could bear it. Immediately I felt great joy and comfort. I saw the death that came from bearing the pain apart from Christ. I found comfort and release as I leaned into Him with my grief, entering into His care and receiving His life in exchange.

Make no mistake about it; the Lord is faithful. He will reveal the extent of the enemy's schemes if we sincerely ask Him to do so: "Death is naked before God; destruction lies uncovered" (Job 26:6).

Reaching Out to Others

Is anyone among you in trouble? He should pray. Is anyone happy? Let him sing songs of praise. Is any one of you sick [without strength, weak, feeble or diseased]? He should call for the elders of the church to pray over him and anoint him with oil in the name of the Lord. And the prayer offered in faith will make the sick person well and the Lord will raise him up. If he has sinned, he will be forgiven. Therefore confess your sins to each other and pray for each other so that you may be healed [made whole]. The prayer of a righteous man is powerful and effective. James 5:13-15

Once I made the decision not to support the destructive influences of the spirit of death, I started getting a little distance from its accompanying thoughts through repeated renunciation. The prayers with brothers and sisters who readily pointed out my "stinkin' thinkin'" became indispensable. Of course, one has to give permission to others to speak into one's life when ungodliness raises its ugly head. But once we do, assertively praying together will send those thoughts and spirits to flight.

Praying *together* is part of the rhythm of living free from the influence of the spirit of death. The enemy's tactic for wearing us down and eliminating us is to separate us from the support of the body of Christ. Think *National Geographic* and the way the lion stalks the lonely gazelle separated from the pack. You get the idea. It would have been impossible without my church family's advocacy for me to overcome that invisible, chronic influence; the power of their prayers has been my lifeline.

Why Prayer With Others is Important

At Embracing Life conferences, trainings, workshops, and in private sessions, we always speak the prayer of renunciation out loud. Why? Our oath is made together as before a "cloud of witnesses." It is a reminder to the enemy that we were not alone in our proclamation. Later on, the enemy (and the old or "false self") will come back with the same old tapes and accusations: "You're not going to pray that again, are you? You did it once, already! You should be beyond that by now!"

Creation will truly live completely free from death's influence the day it is thrown into the lake of fire (Rev. 20:14). Until then, we will have to be vigilant and consistent in renouncing the spirit of death until it no longer finds us an attractive place to hang around. We need courage and ruthless vigilance to engage our will to that end…but we must engage, again and again. Proverbs 15:24 says: "The pathway of life leads upward for the wise to keep him from going down to the grave." We need to build up our spiritual muscle for the climb. Our God will supply all of our strength for the journey in order to fulfill the work he has begun (Phil. 1:6)!

Evicting the Squatters

"Now is the time for judgment on this world; now the prince of this world will be driven out." John 12:31

"Who will rescue me from this body of death? Thanks be to God—through Jesus Christ our Lord!" writes Apostle Paul (Romans 7:24,25). I can state *confidently* that it is possible to live free from the persistent presence of the spirit of death—in all its forms—through the authority of Jesus Christ. You and I will proclaim along with Paul, "Where O death is your sting? Where, O death is your victory?" (1 Cor. 15:55)

Our Father in heaven desires that His children enjoy the increasing fullness of His Presence, unperturbed by the schemes of darkness (Heb. 2:14,15). Everyday He calls us to appropriate, by faith, the abundant life so richly poured out by His Son through the Holy Spirit. When we pray the prayer of renunciation, we are in essence inviting the Lord to clean out the moneychangers within us, His temple. As He goes at it, the Holy Spirit reveals to us the "squatters," if you will, of unrighteousness that are feeding off our unconscious mind. The piercing light and knowledge that can only come from the Lord himself exposes these long-standing parasites. As they are revealed to us, the Lord merely asks us to participate in evicting them. This is much like the children of Israel taking possession of the Promised Land. Although it was legally theirs, after passing through the Jordan (baptism), they entered into and received their inheritance, but still had to do battle to get rid of those who were illegally (from a spiritual standpoint) occupying it. When they made alliances with the inhabitants (whether knowingly or because of deception), it always came back to haunt them. There is a lesson in their example: there can be no false peace with darkness.

This is where pride of thought and image can come to play. Some of us just aren't ready to have that deception exposed. It hurts our pride to think that, as Christians, we could have harbored such thoughts and motives for so long. For others, the idea of darkness and light existing side by side within doesn't fit into their theology (refer to 1 John 1:8-10). Here's a good example of what I'm talking about:

> *Over the years my work as a nurse often involved prayer for the dying. I was at peace with the idea that people on this side of eternity don't live forever, and while mildly curious, I saw no need to pursue the 'spirit of death' thing.... I suppose it was my pride and my stubbornness that resisted the truth—I was in fact living under the influence of the spirit of death. When you began to lead in renouncing the spirit of death, my initial response was, "I don't need this." ...Then I reconsidered, thinking, "I guess I can pray along with this guy. After all, what could it hurt?"*

> *The result was amazing. I had no idea how distorted my thinking had become until a few days after following your lead in renouncing [death]. I realized I no longer obsessed over who would sing what songs and what scriptures would be read at my memorial service. I stopped wondering if I needed to change my will. I quit internally debating whether to have my ashes buried or scattered.*

There may be some of you who have made treaties with illness itself (though you thought it was with God). You asked that a loved one be freed from their illness so that you might carry it instead. This is what is called a substitutionary vow. Though sincerely made, this is sincerely mistaken. Christ is our substitute. He bears our wounds; it is by *His* stripes that we are healed (Isa. 53:4-6). Be Warned. If we ask to be made ill in another's place, the enemy is only too happy to oblige the invitation. The result may be two sick people instead of one. We can carry another's burden in prayer, but we must not take on their illness with it.

I mentioned earlier in my testimony that generational patterns of destructive thought and action were revealed to me in the healing process. For some of you, similar histories may be exposed in prayer such as: premature deaths over generations, recurring illnesses (cancer, heart disease, diabetes), familial curses, criminal activity, occultism and the like. As God surfaces aspects of your family history, it may give you a template for prayer over specific issues.

A final point before we pray. This booklet is intended to be a tool. It is a basic one to assist you in better understanding what *may* have been plaguing you for some time. Even if you are still somewhat unclear as to whether the spirit of death is a serious problem for you—please pray the prayer. It is not a mantra. Edit what you will; it can serve as a framework from which to model a prayer of your own. Use it to pray with others who are struggling with this issue. Pray it OUT LOUD with them. I guarantee you'll be the better for it.

Prayer Essentials: Embracing Life

Preparing to Pray

I have set before you life and death, blessings and curses. Now choose life, so that you and your children may live and that you may love the Lord your God, listen to his voice, and hold fast to him. For the Lord is your life, and he will give you many years in the land... Dt. 30:19, 20

For individuals and groups praying the prayer:

❑ When in a group, have one person (usually the leader) read a short phrase at a time, out loud, with the others repeating it.

❑ If alone, read it out loud. Make your agreement known to God by boldly proclaiming it.

❑ Leave time after finishing the prayer for the Holy Spirit to bring to mind those issues that are specific to you (or when in a group specific to each person). Be encouraged by the knowledge that the Lord is bringing these things up and that one only needs to offer/send them to the cross.

The Prayer

(Pray the following out loud)

I am not born of "natural descent, nor of human decision or a husband's will, but born of God." John 1:13

I am born of "imperishable seed." 1 Peter 1:23

"I can do all things through Christ who strengthens me." Phil. 4:13 (NKJV)

☐ Heavenly Father, Lord Jesus Christ and Holy Spirit, I come before you with my fellow brothers and sisters as witnesses to declare my freedom from the spirit of death and its influences.

☐ By the power and authority granted me by my Lord Jesus Christ, and in whose name I pray, I renounce the spirit of death and all unclean spirits associated with it. I declare any and all attachments, agreements, appeasements and treaties with those spirits nullified and cancelled. Henceforth I will make no false peace with my enemy.

☐ I renounce all identification, activity and preoccupation with suicidal thoughts, death fantasies, illness, despair, hopelessness, perfectionism, fatalism, depression, isolationism, abandonment, passivity, bitterness, rage, anxiety, fear, rejection, violence, racism, witchcraft and medical pronouncements of impending death. Separate them from me, now, Lord, as far as east is from the west.

☐ I sever with the sword of the Spirit of Truth, any attachments to generational spirits going back ten generations, placing the cross of Jesus Christ between me and each one of them.

❑ I repent of any substitutionary agreements, reasserting that it is by Jesus Christ's sacrifice and sufferings that I and my loved ones are saved and healed.

❑ I will make a conscious effort to forgive all those who knowingly or unknowingly wounded me and thereby enabled death to gain influence over me. I ask you Lord to give me ongoing revelation as to whom I need to forgive.

❑ Forgive me Lord for holding unforgiveness, anger, hatred, pride, bitterness, revenge and any other sinful reaction against them. I will continue to release those people and the feelings as you make them known to me.

❑ I receive from you, Lord, the cleansing of your forgiveness in return.

❑ Please continue to reveal any other hidden destructive influences in and over my life, that I may send them to your cross to be nailed there.

❑ I will, by your strength, your love, your power, and in your authority, continue to confess, repent, renounce and resist the spirit of death and its minions, by aligning my will with yours. I proclaim your will for me is to know abundant life.

❑ Now I choose to embrace the fullness of life you have for me, Lord.

❑ I praise you and thank you for always upholding and covering me in your everlasting love.

Amen

In the moments that follow, allow the Lord to surface lingering, dark influences that need to be released to His cross. Wind down the ministry time by praying out loud:

☐ **Jesus, come and make Your authoratative Presence known to me, now, in this place where death has been, and reveal Your life in me.**

The individual or leader should ask the Holy Spirit to seal the work He has done:

☐ **Holy Spirit, I ask you to seal in all you have done and seal out all that I have repented of. Amen.**

In groups, the people may repeat this prayer and the leader will add any other appropriate prayer directives in Jesus' name—especially the need to repeat whenever necessary.

"I am the resurrection and the life. He who believes in me will live even though he dies; and whoever lives and believes in me will never die." John 11:25

Post-prayer Notes for Staying Free

- ❏ Embrace life in the person of Jesus Christ. Open yourself to His wonderful love.

- ❏ Recognize the influence of the spirit of death in your life and ask God to reveal areas that need prayer.

- ❏ Name, confess, and renounce thoughts and feelings that are destructive as often as necessary.

- ❏ Cultivate intimate knowledge of your authority in Christ.

- ❏ Initiate conversations with God and meditate on His Word. Practice His presence (remembering He is always present and will never leave or forsake you) and listen to His healing words. (See suggested readings for listening prayer material.)

- ❏ Write down and meditate on the truth of who you are as revealed in the Word of God and listening prayer.

- ❏ Take opportunity to worship and thank the Lord throughout your day.

- ❏ Stay covered by the prayerful support of others.

- ❏ Pray for others to get free—then "your healing will quickly appear" (Isa. 58:6-12).

- ❏ Remain linked to your church family. Ask God to minister to you when you feel like isolating or clinging to others.

- ❏ Learn to rest in the finished work of Christ; lean on His strength.

- ❏ Keep short accounts: forgive, repent and reconcile.

The one who calls you is faithful and he will do it. (1 Th. 5:24)

Appendix: Fruits of the Holy Spirit vs. Manifestations of the spirit of death

This comparative chart is intended as inspiration for prayer, not a guide for introspection. After reviewing it, you can bring issues that emerge to God in prayer.

Holy Spirit	spirit of death
• Truth	• Lies (or the truth distorted)
• Worship	• Introspection
• Freedom, self control	• Compulsion, bondage
• Balanced view	• Distorted view
• Fruitful, expectations often realized	• Unfruitful, expectations cut off
• Able to make plans and follow through	• Difficulty making and completing plans
• Dreams often fulfilled	• Dreams often unfulfilled or perceived to be unfulfilled.
• Able to cope with frustration and disappointment	• Expects frustration and disappointment
• Embraces life, while aware that death exists.	• Fantasizes about death, dying or suicide, while a vibrant life seems illusive and far off.
• Able to look at health issues objectively and with faith	• Talks about, expects and experiences ill health
• Hope	• Despair, hopelessness
• Compassion	• Narcissism
• Joy	• Depression
• Wholesome sense of humor	• Self-deprecation, cynicism, dark humor
• Mind is clear	• Thoughts and reality seem foggy and gray

Holy Spirit - continued

- Lives in present, while having objectivity about the past and hope for the future
- Victorious through Christ and the cross
- Christ conscious, serving others as God directs
- Knows acceptance & worth, valued because of God's love
- Experiences a range of emotions, from sadness to joy.
- Accepts their own failures and others, without condemnation
- Able to maintain intimate relationships
- Focused on things that are lovely, praiseworthy, of good report
- Able to deal with life through Christ & community.
- Actively exercising will to rest in Christ
- Takes responsibility for mistakes, but doesn't get stuck there

spirit of death - continued

- Lives in past and future, memory is skewed towards negative events
- Victim of fate, others actions
- Self absorbed, sometimes codependent
- Feels rejected and worthless, valued because of what one does or has
- Experiences more negative emotion, sadness, depression, abandonment, helplessness, hopelessness, self-hatred
- Perfectionistic and judgmental, finds forgiving themselves and others difficult
- Finds intimacy illusive.
- Obsessed with thoughts, situations, conversations & media that is dark, centered on crime, death, abuse, heartbreak or violence
- Helpless
- Passive, damaged will
- Blames self and others for situations and reruns offenses and disappointments

Your life and actions may be partially or totally whole, healthy and life-centered in one area and shadowed by death in another. Invite the Lord to continue doing a restorative (sanctifying) work in you as He wills and you are willing.

Bibliography & Suggested Readings

Although not all of the following were directly quoted in the booklet, they have enriched my perspective on embracing life and breaking free from the spirit of death.

Defeating Dark Angels by Charles H. Kraft

The Three Battlegrounds by Francis Frangipane

Listening Prayer by Dave and Linda Olson

Hearing God by Dallas Willard

By My Authority by Charles H. Kraft

Healing Presence by Leanne Payne

Restoring the Christian Soul by Leanne Payne

Embracing Life Ministry Resources

Available online at www.embracinglife.us

Embracing Life Series (ELS) A 14-week, healing discipleship series for persons with life-altering conditions of all kinds. This rich multifaceted workbook is to be used in a group setting and can be read individually – published by *Xulon Press*.

www.EmbracingLife.us

All ELM resources are available on our website. Please visit us for ministry updates on conferences, trainings, groups, and additional resources.

Breaking Free from the spirit of death A booklet based on an expanded version of one of the most impacting chapters from *ELS*. This material explores the various influences of the spirit of death and empowers the reader to hope anew in the promises of abundant life in Christ – published by *Xulon Press*.

More Life! Leaders Guide An eight-week, drop-in group format adapting the materials from *Breaking Free....* This guide is for anyone seeking to lead a group in discovering more of Christ's healing power and abundant life.

Damascus Road **(DVD)** A TBN produced interview with Jonathan Hunter and his testimony.

LaVergne, TN USA
18 September 2009
158359LV00002B/1/P